At Issue

Foodborne Outbreaks

Other Books in the At Issue Series:

At Issue

| Foodborne Outbreaks

Amy Francis, Book Editor

GREENHAVEN PRESS
A part of Gale, Cengage Learning

GALE
CENGAGE Learning·

Farmington Hills, Mich • San Francisco • New York • Waterville, Maine
Meriden, Conn • Mason, Ohio • Chicago

Judy Galens, *Manager, Frontlist Acquisitions*

© 2016 Greenhaven Press, a part of Gale, Cengage Learning.

Gale and Greenhaven Press are registered trademarks used herein under license.

For more information, contact:
Greenhaven Press
27500 Drake Rd.
Farmington Hills, MI 48331-3535
Or you can visit our Internet site at gale.cengage.com

For product information and technology assistance, contact us at

Gale Customer Support, 1-800-877-4253
For permission to use material from this text or product, submit all requests online at www.cengage.com/permissions

Further permissions questions can be e-mailed to permissionrequest@cengage.com

Articles in Greenhaven Press anthologies are often edited for length to meet page requirements. In addition, original titles of these works are changed to clearly present the main thesis and to explicitly indicate the author's opinion. Every effort is made to ensure that Greenhaven Press accurately reflects the original intent of the authors. Every effort has been made to trace the owners of copyrighted material.

LIBRARY OF CONGRESS CATALOGING-IN-PUBLICATION DATA

Names: Francis, Amy, editor.
Title: Foodborne outbreaks / Amy Francis, book editor.
Description: Farmington Hills, Mich : Greenhaven Press, a part of Gale, Cengage Learning, [2016] | Series: At issue | Includes bibliographical references and index.
Identifiers: LCCN 2015028073 | ISBN 9780737774061 (hardback) | ISBN 9780737774078 (paperback)
Subjects: LCSH: Foodborne diseases. | Food--Microbiology. | Food industry and trade--Safety measures. | BISAC: JUVENILE NONFICTION / Health & Daily Living / Diseases, Illnesses & Injuries.
Classification: LCC QR201.F62 F674 2016 | DDC 615.9/54--dc23
LC record available at http://lccn.loc.gov/2015028073

Printed in the United States of America

-1 0 1 2 3   21 20 19 18 17

Contents

Introduction

The National School Lunch Act was signed into law by President Harry Truman in 1946. The Act promised to provide nutritionally balanced, affordable lunches to school children across the country each day. As written, the Act was passed "to safeguard the health and well-being of the Nation's children and to encourage the domestic consumption of nutritious agricultural commodities and other food."

Since then multiple studies have credited the National School Lunch Program with a reduction in malnutrition, increased school attendance, and improved learning and test scores. While many assume the food provided through the program must meet minimum government quality standards, the safety of school lunches has been called into question following several reports of illness outbreaks. Examples include flour tortillas that were to blame for an outbreak in Massachusetts in 2003, salmonella that sickened children in five different Chicago schools in 2012, and a beet salad that left twenty-two children ill in a Maine school in 2015.

All in all, as reported by ABC News last year, sixteen thousand students were sickened by foodborne illnesses from school lunches over the last decade, and the annual number of students sickened has risen each year. As part of an ABC News *Primetime* investigation, reporters inspecting schools found "dead rodents just feet from where food was being prepared, roaches crawling along filthy floors, dishwashers that don't clean children's trays, and food being kept at temperatures where potentially dangerous bacteria can thrive." Additionally, hidden news cameras recorded the conditions inside a plant that continued processing chicken for schools even after failing repeated salmonella tests. Among their findings were "chickens with yellow sores . . . potentially hazardous fecal matter . . . filth in machines that box chicken and processing equipment dripping with chicken fat."[1]

In fact, Grace Chen, reporting in *Public School Review*, found school lunches had less stringent health standards than many fast food restaurants, putting kids at risk for hazardous pathogens. She writes, "Some reports suggest that fast-food restaurants actually check for bacteria and pathogens between five and ten times more often" than are done with school lunch meats. Chen went on to say that "there were cases where the Agricultural Marketing Service (AMS), which purchases meat for schools, bought meats with pathogen and E. coli levels which even exceeded acceptable levels for fast-food outlets."[2]

A bag lunch from home might sound like the best solution to ensure a safe lunch, but there can be problems with packed lunches, too. Linda Carroll, reporting for *Today Health*, states that most kids' lunches, even those with ice packs, aren't keeping the food cool enough to prevent bacteria from growing. "Ninety percent of the 705 preschooler sack lunches tested by University of Texas scientists," she writes, "had risen to temperatures considered too high to prevent the growth of bacteria."[3] Additionally, for the many students who rely on free or reduced-cost school lunch, bringing a lunch from home is not even an option.

U.S. News & World Report author Ann Cooper says it is important not to forget these kids. She writes, "All children, regardless of their circumstances, deserve safe, nourishing and delicious school meals. When we abandon school food, we

---

1. "How Safe Are School Lunches?," ABC News, November 7, 2014. http://abcnews.go.com/Primetime/story?id=132030.
2. Grace Chen, "Why Fast Food Is 'Healthier' Than School Lunches: The Shocking USDA Truth," *Public School Review*, June 16, 2015. http://www.publicschoolreview.com/blog/why-fast-food-is-healthier-than-school-lunches-the-shocking-usda-truth.
3. Linda Carroll, "9 Out of 10 Preschoolers' Lunches Reach Unsafe Temperatures," *Today Health*, August 8, 2011. http://www.today.com/id/44039875/ns/today-today_health/t/out-preschoolers-lunches-reach-unsafe-temperatures.

abandon children who could benefit from our powerful voices, our influence, and our strength: three things that children—especially poor ones—lack."[4]

Wisconsin state representative Warren Petryk acknowledges the risk and believes something can be done to help make school lunches safer for everyone. He sponsored a bill in Wisconsin that would require schools to meet the same requirements as restaurants before serving meals to students. Petryk stated that approximately 125 million meals are served in Wisconsin schools annually and that the risk of a foodborne illness outbreak is high.

We know, however, that restaurants aren't immune from spreading foodborne illnesses—neither are farms, processors, nor supermarkets. The state of food safety and the best methods for reducing foodborne outbreaks and improving food delivery from farm to plate is debated by the authors in the following pages of *At Issue: Foodborne Outbreaks*.

4. Ann Cooper, "School Lunch: Opting Out Is Not an Option," *U.S. News & World Report*, April 28, 2015. http://health.usnews.com/health-news/blogs/eat-run/2015/04/28/school-lunch-opting-out-is-not-an-option.

1

Progress Has Been Made Toward Reducing Foodborne Outbreaks

Yasmine Motarjemi

Yasmine Motarjemi holds degrees in food science and technology from the University of Languedoc, Montpellier, France, and food engineering from the University of Lund, Sweden.

Infectious diseases are commonly spread by food, particularly in developing nations. Concern for food safety in the light of increased trade led to two important World Trade Organization agreements on safety in food imports, and food safety has continued to improve through these agreements. Additionally, increased awareness of foodborne illnesses, additional research, better legislation, improved food quality systems with enhanced alerts and traceability, better training for food safety officials, and educational campaigns for the general public have also improved the safety of our food supply.

Today, April 7, 2015, is World Health Day. This year, the World Health Organization is dedicating this day to "food safety." The year 2015 is also the twentieth anniversary of the World Trade Organization (WTO), the creation of which (in 1995) had a major impact on food safety; it promoted the subject on the health, economic and political agendas. During the last two to three decades, the world has been the arena of numerous food safety crisis and untold numbers of incidents of food contamination or foodborne disease outbreaks. Many of these, particularly in developing countries, never come to the attention of the public health authorities, much less the general public. Nevertheless, major progress has been made in food safety management, even though lessons learned were to the cost of many incidents, where people have been injured or lost their lives.

A Glimpse into the Past

Food safety has been of concern to humankind since the dawn of history. In early times, the major concern and threat to survival of humans was probably the consumption of poisonous foods. It is presumed that primitive humans used their sensory perceptions, that is, taste and smell, together with memory to evaluate the safety of their food. In other words, consumers would directly taste the food and would, through trial and error, learn which ones were safe and which ones were to be avoided.

Until the 1970–80s, in many countries, food safety remained as an empirical science, principally, based on codes of good practices.

As civilization progressed, in many cultures, religious rules prescribed food handling practices that protected people from certain foodborne diseases. However, the flourishing of trade gave rise to concerns for food adulteration and fraud and coming into force of first laws. For centuries progress was slow.

A turning point in the history of food safety was the discovery and utilization of microscopes by Anton von Leeuwenhoek (1632–1723) who first reported seeing microbes. He called these "animalcules." Later in the nineteenth century, the work of scientists such as Louis Pasteur (1822–1895) who developed the germ theory, and Robert Koch (1843–1910) known for the criteria that establish the causal relationship between a pathogen and an illness, set the foundation of modern food hygiene and food microbiology. Advances in science and technology in the last 200 years led to new methods of food preservations. Some like canning or spray drying were initially for military purposes. These methods were instrumental in transforming lifestyle and set the ground for industrialization of food production. Scientific developments in analytical techniques have also been an important impetus in the development of food safety, as they have increased scientists understanding of biological hazards, their ecology and their methods of control.

In spite of this progress, until the 1970–80s, in many countries, food safety remained as an empirical science, principally, based on codes of good practices. As many prevalent infectious diseases, for example, cholera, shigellosis, typhoid and paratyphoid fevers, were attributed to the use of unsafe water or poor sanitation, the use of unsafe water was the main concern and the codes focused principally on sanitary measures. The management of food establishments was also heavily based on visual inspection, and sometimes on subjective judgments. As laboratory techniques developed, microbiological or chemical testing of food products came to complement visual inspection and formed the basis for food safety management. Where these measures have been implemented, they have been effective in preventing and reducing diseases such as cholera and typhoid and paratyphoid fevers for which water plays a central role in their spread in the environment. However, they have been insufficient to prevent other types of foodborne diseases, some of which increased dramatically.

Defying Challenges

In the mid-1980s and 1990s, with the increase in foodborne diseases and a number of adverse food safety events, public health authorities realized the magnitude of the challenges that they were facing, namely:

• A substantial increase in a number of foodborne diseases such as salmonellosis, campylobacteriosis, listeriosis, *E. coli* *O157*, etc., and the serious and chronic health consequences of these.

• Increased likelihood of large-scale foodborne disease out-breaks, due to industrialization and mass production.

• Emergence of new pathogenic agents such as enterohem-orrhagic *E. coli*, *Campylobacter* spp. and opportunistic patho-gens such as *Cryptosporidium*, *Listeria monocytogenes*, *Crono-bacter sakazakii* (previously *Enterbobacter sakazakii*).

• Increased concern for the health effects of chemical con-taminants and environmental pollution.

• An increase in the number of vulnerable population, in particular immunocompromised individuals and the elderly.

• Urbanization and changes in lifestyles with subsequent increases in the number of out-of-home meals and a growing number of establishments for food services and work can-teens.

In Europe, a wave of several food safety crises, notably the BSE [bovine spongiform encephalopathy] crisis in 1996 and 2000, and the dioxin crisis in 1999, revealed gaps in food safety management.

• An increase in international trade in food and travel with the risk of importing contaminated food or infected persons.

• International recognition of the role of food contamina-tion in infant diarrhea and its association with malnutrition received.

• The recognition of the role of professional and domestic food handlers in food safety and the need for the education and training [this poses a tremendous challenge to educate (and/or train) an entire population, as any member of the population is a potential food handler, with the exception of newborns].

Parallel to these developments, a number of adverse events contributed to an increased concern. Among these:

• The cholera epidemic in Latin America and Africa in the 1990s raised the awareness of the governments of the developing countries on the importance of food safety management; countries who were affected by cholera saw their food export embargoed for food safety reasons. Later, the European Union extended their food import embargo to all those countries that could not demonstrate adequate capabilities in controlling the safety of their food supply.

• In Europe, a wave of several food safety crises, notably the BSE [bovine spongiform encephalopathy, also known as mad cow disease] crisis in 1996 and 2000, and the dioxin crisis in 1999, revealed gaps in food safety management. Worldwide outbreaks of foodborne diseases caused by pathogens, such as *Salmonella*, enterohemorrhagic *E. coli* and *L. monocytogenes*, alerted the general public. Subsequently, a general atmosphere of mistrust developed in many western countries. This in turn affected the acceptance of novel technologies such as biotechnology, food irradiation, or industrial methods of food preservation such as the use of food additives.

• Concomitant with the increased public concern, the finalization of the Uruguay Round of Multilateral Negotiations in Marrakesh and the establishment of the WTO in 1995 paved the way for increased trade in food and feed, and raised concerns about the eventual import of contaminated food and feed. To provide countries with the right for protection of their populations without establishing unnecessary discriminatory regulations, two agreements came into force with the establishment of WTO. These agreements were 1) Agreement on the Application of Sanitary and Phytosanitary Measures (SPS) and 2) Agreement on the Technical Barriers to Trade.

These agreements also included concepts such as appropriate level of health protection, risk assessment, equivalence, etc., which required further clarification.

In this climate of public concern, a number of questions were raised and debated among stakeholders:

- How safe should food be?

- What should the appropriate level of protection be?

- To what level should hazards in food be controlled?

- Who decides and what data should be considered in the decision-making process?

- How are consistency, objectivity, acceptability and efficiency ensured?

- How efficient and cost-effective is a control measure and at what point of the food chain should a hazard be controlled and at what cost?

- How are feasibilities and other risks factors considered in the decisions?

- How will food safety be controlled in the global market?

The WTO/SPS agreements ... contributed to the development of a number of food safety principles.

From their perspective, consumers represented by the consumer organizations also raised questions such as:

- Who is deciding? And on what basis?

- How is the uncertainty considered in the decision-making processes?

- How are stakeholders' views taken into account?

- How are the societal values considered?

These questions gave rise to the principles and concepts such as transparency, precautionary principles and involvement of stakeholders in the decision-making process, and considering scientific and social values in this process.

Food safety incidents, such as BSE and dioxin mentioned above, also raise the importance of:

- The 'Farm to Fork' approach

- The consideration of science and uncertainty in science in the process

- Transparency in decision-making

- The impact of perception on the food supply

The WTO/SPS agreements also contributed to the development of a number of food safety principles. Among others, it required that regulations follow a certain number of principles, namely:

- Be based on sound scientific assessment of the risk

- Be nondiscriminatory

- Be transparent

- Accept equivalent approaches to achieve the same level of health protection

Additionally, the WTO referred to the standards, practices and other recommendations of the Codex Alimentarius Commission (CAC) as representing international consensus regarding health and safety requirements for food. In other words, the SPS agreement recognized the CAC as a reference for international requirements for food safety. This meant that countries that rejected food which complied with the Codex food safety standards had to provide scientific evidence that the food in question posed a specific risk for their population. Indirectly, this encouraged countries to align their legislation with the standards of CAC. Short of this, they could be challenged by the exporting country, and eventually required by a WTO Dispute Settlement Panel to provide scientific evidence, that is, risk assessment data, for having a legislation that is more stringent than the standards and recommendations of CAC. An illustrative example of the application of this article was the case of hormones in beef for which European countries had to provide evidence of risk before a WTO Dispute Settlement Panel.

Undoubtedly the management of food safety and hygiene in the food chain has improved.

These developments at the international level and the increased awareness of the general public led to numerous changes in the management of food safety. In the food industry, the Hazard Analysis and Critical Control Points (HACCP) system and traceability received heightened attention, and in some countries, it became mandatory. At the governmental level, risk analysis emerged as a decision-making process. In some countries or regions, it led to the restructuring of governmental institutions. For instance, in Europe, the European Food Safety Authority was established in 2002 as a result of this. . . .

Future Outlook

Today, concepts such as HACCP and risk analysis have been well developed and integrated in the management of food safety and hygiene at national and international levels. Codes of good practices have become much more robust. Laboratory and analytical methods have advanced significantly and become routine. Communication with consumers and consideration of their perceptions in decision making process has become the *modern modus operandi* of governments. Crisis management has become much more proficient.

One of the key developments in the recent year has been the recognition of the need for an integrated approach to management of food safety and hygiene, particularly in consideration of industry practices. Subsequently, private standards such as ISO 22000 have been developed to allow for a more thorough and efficient verification of food operations.

Undoubtedly the management of food safety and hygiene in the food chain has improved. Today, the food safety community has all the tools and elements to provide a safe food for the population. Nevertheless a number of challenges remain:

• Quantitative risk assessment as a basis for decision-making is still in its infancy. New concepts such as food safety objectives and performances objectives have been developed, however except in a few cases, they are not yet widely applied.

• Toxicological evaluation of chemical hazards, in particular, long-term exposure to low doses and/or their interactions, as well as their monitoring in the food supply, needs to continue with a high degree of vigilance and impartiality.

• The food industry is still struggling in implementing management systems such as HACCP, partly because food operations, be they large or small, have each their complexity. Application of HACCP, as it was envisaged, meet enormous difficulties. This is partly because HACCP is very time consuming and management of many companies fail to provide the necessary expertise, time investment and/or human resources. These gaps stem for the fact that often food safety is taken for granted and the true needs for ensuring food safety are underestimated and are not recognized at their fair value.

• In some operations, the application of basic hygiene continues to be substandard; food service operations in the developing countries remain a particular concern. This is a threat to the local population, as well as travelers and international trade.

• There has been an increase in incidence of fraud and adulteration of food. The unpredictable nature of such events renders their prevention and management very difficult. Whistleblowing is perhaps the most efficient way for preventing or limiting fraud as well as mismanagement or misconduct in food safety. Considering the globalization of the food supply and the likelihood of importing contaminated products from exporting countries, legislation on whistleblowing needs to be harmonized among countries.

• The concern for emergence of new pathogens, acts of sabotage, tampering or counterfeit products will continue to loom.

• Climatic changes and subsequent environmental disasters (e.g., floods) will also contribute to the emergence of new threats or contamination of the environment. The implications of these for the safety of the food supply, particularly agricultural products, need to be anticipated.

• Similarly, demographical changes, their impact on food security as well as socio-economic situations of countries will continue to influence food safety standards and practices, and related public health outcomes.

• Investigation of outbreaks, and their root cause analysis up to the level of management of companies, still need to be developed and reinforced. Short of this, outbreaks will be repeated as was the case with several incidences of Salmonella in peanut butter in United States, or melamine in the U.S. (2007) and China (2008). It is important that the outcomes of investigations of incidents are shared with the entire community of food professionals.

• More attention should be given to the health and safety of operators, as their health conditions can impact safety of products and services in multiple ways. Communicable illness in food handlers can be a source of contamination of food. However, other factors such as burnout, overwork, stress, mistreatment and abuse of staff can also increase the risk of human error, accidental contamination or deliberate sabotage, for example, tampering.

• There is also a need for governmental agencies to be more proactive with regard to whistleblowing cases, and not only encourage whistleblowing but also protect whistleblowers against retaliation, as reparation of injustice made to them is difficult and insignificant compared to the prejudice they undergo. Fear of retaliation will silence whistleblowers, which play essential roles in prevention of mismanagement and negligence.

• Finally, a question for the future is what the Trans-Pacific Partnership Agreement and The Trade in Services Agreement will bring about, and how they impact the safety standard of our supply?

2

Progress Has Not Been Made Toward Reducing Foodborne Outbreaks

Elizabeth Grossman

Elizabeth Grossman is a journalist and writer specializing in environmental and science issues. She is the author of Chasing Molecules, High Tech Trash, Watershed, *and other books.*

The foodborne illness outbreaks of 2006 from E. coli *resulted in the Food Safety Modernization Act (FSMA); however, the FSMA is still a work in progress and all of the rules have not yet been set. Nine years later, a foodborne illness from spinach contaminated with* Listeria *raises questions about how much food safety has improved. Information about food origination is still lacking as is legislation requiring companies to issue recalls quickly. Without this important legislation fully in place, new outbreaks will continue to occur.*

Over the past two weeks [beginning late March 2015], grocery stores in every region of the United States and Canada have been taking frozen organic spinach—and a host of products ranging from frozen dinners to spinach dip—off their shelves. All the spinach in question, which may have been contaminated with *Listeria*, comes from a single California-based vegetable processing company.

No illnesses have been reported, but the massive recall has affected about half a dozen companies including Amy's Kitchen and Rising Moon Organics and major retailers, among them, Target, Costco, Wegmans, and Giant Eagle. For many, it brings to mind the infamous *E. coli* recall that rocked the U.S. produce industry, killed three people, and sickened 205 in 2006. And it raises the question: Has our food gotten any safer in the past nine years?

"That outbreak was a watershed for the fresh produce industry. Not just leafy greens but all produce," says United Fresh Produce Association Senior Vice President for Food Safety and Technology, David Gombas.

Traceability—the ability to trace food from kitchen table back to its origins and locate the source of a problem if one occurs—is key to maintaining a safe food supply.

As leafy greens eaters may remember, in 2006, *E. coli* O157:H7 was traced to spinach that was grown and bagged in California and then sold all across North America. While scientists and regulators determined that the contamination was caused by animals in the field, the precise source was never definitively pinpointed.

Food Safety Modernization Act

The incident prompted new voluntary food safety guidelines for companies that sell leafy greens in California, the state that produces most of the nation's lettuce and spinach. It also played a role in the creation of a major piece of federal legislation—the Food Safety Modernization Act (FSMA)—the (underfunded) rules of which the U.S. Food and Drug Administration (FDA) is still finalizing.

At the time, says Gombas, many produce industry leaders came to realize, "that a whole lot of information was missing" about the food we eat. "Not only on leafy greens but for fresh produce in general."

Traceability—the ability to trace food from kitchen table back to its origins and locate the source of a problem if one occurs—is key to maintaining a safe food supply. And while there have been quite a few measures to improve quick identification of steps in the produce supply chain—who's sold what to whom and when—some important information is still inaccessible to the food-buying public.

In the case of the current spinach recall, Coastal Green, the company that processed and sold the greens to other companies which turned it into to packaged frozen and ready-to-steam spinach or who used it in ready-to-cook or frozen pasta or dips, has been readily identified. But the grower(s) have not been. Nor is there any information available on where exactly the spinach was grown, not even from the FDA.

Since food companies do their own internal food testing, it's typically up to food processors and retailers to notify the FDA [concerning issues of contaminated food].

While some preventative measures—like basic hygiene for everyone who touches the produce—are relatively simple to achieve, identifying sources of contamination in the field is more difficult, Gombas explains. "By the time you get a positive detection, you're days away from when the contamination event occurred," he says.

But when it comes to *Listeria*, the pathogen in the current spinach recall, the "bug can occur at different points in the system, on the farm or in processing, so you need different precautions," says Christopher Waldrop, director of the Consumer Federation of America's Food Policy Institute. And like other food-related bacterial infections, *Listeria* is of increasing concern given the rise in antibiotic resistance.

Faster Reporting Is Needed

"Ideally, as soon as a company finds out it has a problem, they should be letting their customers know and letting the public know. There shouldn't be a time lag," says Waldrop. But, he notes, the rules about when a company issues a recall are not dictated by law. "It's all voluntary," he says.

While the 2002 Bioterrorism Response and Preparedness Act requires food companies to keep sales records, the FDA's requirements are not yet finalized. Several "pilot" traceability projects are now underway under FSMA to "explore and evaluate methods to rapidly and effectively identify recipients of food to prevent or mitigate a foodborne illness outbreak."

Since food companies do their own internal food testing, it's typically up to food processors and retailers to notify the FDA, which posts recall notices on its website and distributes them via email. The companies are then supposed to notify customers, but there aren't any specific timeframes required by regulation.

Coastal Green "is conducting this recall voluntarily," the FDA explained in an email. But the agency also stresses, "a recall action is a voluntary action on the part of the firm, unless mandated by FDA," which would happen only in an urgent situation—if a serious contamination issue is confirmed—or the company has somehow failed to act.

In the current recall, processors and distributors receiving the spinach quickly notified food companies so products could be pulled from store shelves. "We immediately alerted FDA—it was the same afternoon (Friday, March 20 [2015]) that we received the notice from Coastal," says a spokesperson for Amy's Kitchen.

"We have to follow where every ingredient goes in every product," says Mark Hubbard spokesman for Twin City Foods, a processing, packing, and distribution company affected by the recall. Thanks to the changes that have occurred over the last decade, companies like his have a system for doing so. Hubbard calls the change, "a good thing."

John Personeni, president of the Carmel Food Group which owns the Rising Moon Organics brand is not quite so sanguine. He says his company purchased the spinach in question for ravioli in December of last year [2014], but wasn't notified of a problem until March [2015]. "We're usually notified much sooner. That's why this is so disturbing," he says.

The FDA, which is investigating the problem, had no additional specifics to offer in response to our questions. And it's not clear what—if any—additional information will be available in the weeks to come. Coastal Greens did not respond to requests for information and its website does not list spinach among the company's products.

The big questions, says Waldrop are: "How do we prevent this from happening again?" and "Would the [FSMA] rules that are coming out of FDA have prevented it from happening?"

The existing voluntary California leafy greens guidelines and the forthcoming FSMA rules include safety standards for things like irrigation water, manure use, equipment, and facilities. But ensuring food safety at the source also involves training and empowering farmworkers to report problems. Peter O'Driscoll, director of the Equitable Food Initiative, a private-public partnership that aims to improve working conditions on farms, says his organization is doing just that.

"One of the growers we work with instituted something they call red-button moments," explains Waldrop whose organization is an Equitable Food Initiative member. "Any worker can stop the production line at any time."

But not all farms have such a policy. And poor working conditions on farms are often associated with food safety issues. For example, Jensen Farms—the large Colorado cantaloupe grower responsible for the 2011 *Listeria* outbreak that killed 33 people—was fined the very same year for providing their workers with substandard, unsanitary housing.

"The really good news is while the [recall] was widespread," cases "of illness or problems are nonexistent as far as we can tell," says Hubbard.

But just how much of that outcome is due to luck, versus the product of recent changes, is still hard to gauge.

3

The Federal Food Safety Modernization Act Is Underfunded

Michael Taylor

Michael Taylor is deputy commissioner of foods and veterinary medicine for the US Food and Drug Administration.

The Federal Food Safety Modernization Act (FSMA) is key to establishing and maintaining a safer food supply. The need to adequately fund the program is urgent due to the number of imports—the largest source of safety problems. Also, the FSMA rules will be in place and mandated by the government, so the money necessary to implement the Act is essential. Without it, there will be more illnesses and the industry will continue to be disrupted, further endangering the food supply.

We all knew FSMA [Food Safety Modernization Act] was a big deal when Congress passed it a little over four years ago. After a decade of illness outbreaks, import safety problems, and market disruptions that shook consumer confidence and imposed billions of dollars in costs on the food system, Congress mandated a paradigm shift to prevention—to establishing a modern system of food safety protection based not on reacting to problems but on preventing them from happening in the first place. That's how we'll achieve the food safety goals we all share—fewer illnesses, stronger consumer confidence in the system of protection, and a level playing field for American farmers and food companies.

In addition to embracing these goals, Congress adopted a strong vision of how to achieve them. With broad input and support from industry and consumers alike, Congress said that a food safety system fit for the 21st century must be built on what the food industry itself has learned about how to make food safe and how to manage global supply chains, and it must harness the efforts of all food system participants—public and private, domestic and foreign—in a collaborative effort to see that those practical, effective, preventive measures are consistently followed.

We want to use the new FSMA framework to achieve good food safety results through collaborative effort, rather than focusing on the traditional enforcement approaches that were our main tool before FSMA was enacted.

Fundamental Changes

As big as that sounds—and it's by far the biggest overhaul of the food safety system since the first national law was passed over a century ago—I don't think any of us fully envisioned how much would have to be done and how much would have to change to make FSMA a success. The law itself spelled out the large number of regulations FDA must issue to establish the prevention framework. Indeed, FSMA made FDA [Food and Drug Administration] responsible for some 50 specific deliverables in the form of rules, guidance for industry, new programs, and reports to Congress. FDA has been hard at work on these, with the major rules set to be final this year under court-ordered deadlines. . . .

But we've learned that FSMA is about far more than new rules. It's about how FDA changes fundamentally its approach to implementing food safety rules, including how FDA works with other governments and the food industry to achieve food safety success. That's why FDA has devoted such huge effort over the past two years to rethinking every aspect of what will go into achieving high rates of compliance with the FSMA rules—for both home-grown and imported food—compliance that is essential to food safety *and* to achieving the level playing field on food safety that American consumers and industry both demand.

For example, because we know that the vast majority of American farmers and food companies want to do the right thing on food safety and want to comply with the new rules, we are basing our FSMA implementation strategy on the principle of "educate before and while we regulate." This means providing guidance and technical assistance to industry so they know what's expected and are supported in doing it. It also means reorienting and retraining the FDA inspection and compliance workforce, as well as our state food safety partners, to work in this new way so we can provide consistent, high-quality oversight within the more technically sophisticated FSMA framework.

We want to use the new FSMA framework to achieve good food safety results through collaborative effort, rather than focusing on the traditional enforcement approaches that were our main tool before FSMA was enacted. We will of course enforce vigorously when that's what's needed to protect consumers, but the goal is food safety, not enforcement cases. . . .

The FSMA paradigm shift and the change needed to succeed are especially urgent and especially evident when it comes to imported food. The volume of imports is vast and growing, and the number of foreign manufacturing facilities registered to sell food in the United States is greater than the number of U.S. facilities. Safety problems with imported foods were one of the main drivers of FSMA's enactment, and Congress recognized that the old system of relying almost entirely on FDA inspectors to detect and correct food safety problems by examining food at the border is drastically outmoded.

Congress thus mandated a new import safety system that harnesses the capacity and responsibility of importers to manage their supply chains to ensure imports meet our new FSMA standards. And it directed FDA to increase its foreign presence through more foreign inspections and more engagement with foreign governments to leverage their food safety efforts.

Enactment of [President Obama's] request for a budget authority increase of $109.5 million for FY 2016 would make it possible for FDA to move forward in 2016 toward successful implementation of FSMA.

Funding the Program

All of this of course costs money. The Congressional Budget Office (CBO) estimated that, to implement FSMA effectively, FDA would need a cumulative increase in its base funding for food safety of $583 million over the first five years following enactment. In those five years, FY [fiscal year] 2011–2015, we've received much-appreciated base increases totaling $162 million, which have been crucial for getting FSMA implementation off the ground.

During this period, FDA has made its own estimates of the FSMA funding need, as explained in a brief summary of the history and context of FSMA funding we recently posted. And we did this in full recognition of the fiscal challenges facing the government and with a commitment to be as targeted and cost effective as we can be. For example, we are not building a new system on top of the old but rather redeploying our current workforce and resources to implement FSMA and our new compliance strategy. We are prioritizing investments that leverage public and private resources and that support our industry and state partners in playing their food safety roles.

And we are driving change within FDA to improve efficiency. This includes the Commissioner's game-changing initiative to vertically integrate and streamline the collaboration between our experts and policymakers in headquarters and our field-based inspection and compliance workforce.

The bottom line is that with program efficiencies we can gain, plus the FSMA funding increases FDA has received to date, enactment of the President's request for a budget authority increase of $109.5 million for FY 2016 would make it possible for FDA to move forward in 2016 toward successful implementation of FSMA.

We think the request is modest in relation to the benefits FSMA promises for consumers and the food system and given what it takes to both revamp everything we've done in the past and take on such major new tasks as implementing the first-ever national standards for produce safety and building a new import safety system.

And the request is modest in relation to CBO's original estimate of FSMA funding needs. With the full $109.5 million in new budget authority, our total FSMA funding increases would still be less than half of what CBO estimated is needed for success.

Finally, and crucially, FDA's 2016 budget request reflects the unavoidable fact that the future is now when it comes to FSMA implementation. Let me explain what I mean by that. At the end of this year, we *will* have new FSMA rules—we are committed and we are under court order. By the end of 2016, we will begin overseeing their implementation, and we will do that in large part through legally mandated FSMA inspections of food facilities. Those inspections *will* happen.

Thus, in terms of preparing for effective and efficient FSMA implementation, the future is here. If we invest properly in 2016 to prepare FDA and the industry for success, we will have success, in the form of better food safety, stronger public confidence, and a level playing field for U.S. farmers and food companies. If we don't invest properly in 2016, food safety will suffer—people will get sick who wouldn't otherwise—and the food industry will be disrupted—large and small operators alike—for lack of guidance and technical assistance for industry and lack of consistent, technically well-supported inspection by FDA and the states.

That is what is at stake in FDA's 2016 FSMA funding request.

4

The Global Food System Increases Foodborne Outbreaks

William Marler, interviewed by Cynthia Graber

Cynthia Graber is a print and radio journalist covering science, technology, agriculture, and food. William Marler is a food safety lawyer.

The easiest way to make the food supply safer is to simplify the food process so that there are fewer opportunities for food contamination. For example, people used to be limited to local produce, but now food is imported to make most items available year-round. The additional food imports make the food system more complex, and as a result most outbreaks occur in food highly processed and transported long distances. Additionally, there aren't enough inspectors to visit all of the produce processing plants. The most important step, therefore, is to limit the steps from farm to table so as to reduce the chances for food to become contaminated.

This is Cynthia Graber reporting for FutureFood 2050. Food safety in the U.S. is still a huge issue today. According to the Centers for Disease Control [and Prevention (CDC)], 48 million Americans a year are sickened by foodborne illnesses, which leads to 128,000 hospitalizations and

3,000 deaths. In addition to the loss of life, the government estimates the cost from such illnesses in the billions of dollars in terms of lost wages and productivity and medical expenses.

William Marler is a well-known lawyer whose practice, Marler Clark, is called The Food Safety Law Firm. He's won a number of key lawsuits that have advanced food policy in the U.S. In one of his most famous, he won a landmark case for victims of E. coli contamination from hamburgers purchased at Jack in the Box restaurants in 1993. I asked him about the current state of food safety.

I think we really have to ask ourselves about how complex do we really need to make food.

Complex Food Economy

WILLIAM MARLER: There's a lot of things going on sort of simultaneously. I mean, you know, these bugs are constantly evolving. They're dealing with more virulence than we've seen—you know, especially in bugs like antibiotic-resistant salmonellas and Listeria. These are kind of bugs that we didn't see 30 years ago, so you have to really look a lot at how food is produced and then balance that against, you know, a growing world population. And it does make it very complex. And then when you add on to that 25, 30 years ago, you know, you couldn't get bananas certain times of the year. Now you get them whenever you want them. And so food's coming in from all over the world. So, I mean, it's a global food economy. It's difficult to control, and human beings are not necessarily the best at dealing with very, very complex problems. And the food system has become incredibly complex.

GRABER: So what do you think some of the biggest holes in the system are, both here and overseas?

I think we really have to ask ourselves about how complex do we really need to make food. Do we really have to have bagged salad 12 months of the year? I mean, you look at the outbreaks that have occurred—the large outbreaks. They're usually in highly processed products that are shipped long distances. So when you're trying to figure out ways to make your food supply safer, sometimes simpler is better. Now that doesn't necessarily mean that local organic grown products are not going to sicken you if that local farmer is not using good manufacturing processes. But the more a product is manufactured, remanufactured, shipped, and you having cold-chain issues and keeping things hot or keeping things cold, it just makes for the entry of a bacterium or a virus into that process that can cause people to get sick.

There's always new interventions and innovations. . . . We've seen that once the government made the decision that you could not have E. coli in hamburger, the industry figured out a way to try to eradicate it.

So based on what you said, it seems like there are a few different things. You mentioned kind of too many steps in the processing and the cold chain in which, you know, bugs can kind of grow and proliferate. Is it also an issue that there aren't enough inspectors or that there are no repercussions for, um, food safety issues?

Let me, let me give you an example. If you look at Food Safety Inspection Service, which is the FSIS, it's the USDA [US Department of Agriculture], it's the meat side of the food equation, um. That was an entity that really grew up, you know, at the post-Upton Sinclair "The Jungle." And, and you have an inspector in every plant. And they're public employees and they're in the plant. They're monitoring what's going on, um. But yet we still had the horrific E. coli outbreaks in the '90s and, you know, early part of the 2000s, even though that product was being inspected. But we had not brought sort of the new technologies of testing meat and test-and-hold and, and interventions to get E. coli off the meat.

Those things still had not been sort of implemented. Once those things got implemented, you know, we've seen a dramatic decrease in, in the number of E. coli cases linked to red meat and hamburger. And that's a good thing. The FDA side of the ledger is, you know, everything else. It's fish. It's vegetables, cereals, you know, and imports—non-meat. They don't have inspectors, and some of the worst foodborne illness outbreaks that I've been involved in, the plants that I got court orders to go into, had never been visited by an FDA inspector, ever. And so we've created this sort of enormous food manufacturing industry, all of which really has sort of come about post-World War II. And we really don't have sort of the level of inspection that is, I think, required even though we still mandate companies to do food safety planning and testing and, you know, recall.

I really feel strongly that you've got to have a public employee in the plant or at least inspecting the plants on a regular basis. And that's just a real failure on the part of, you know, our government to do that and, frankly, the taxpayer to pay for it.

Interventions and Innovations for Food Safety

You mentioned technology. Are there technological innovations or developments that you think, you know, that you see coming down the pipe that will help make consumers safer?

There's always new interventions and innovations. You know, we've seen that once the government made the decision that you could not have E. coli in hamburger, the industry figured out a way to try to eradicate it, and they did it by a variety of interventions, um, and cleaning up the process of the slaughter plant. And again, we've seen O157, that nasty form of E. coli, just almost disappear from the meat side of the equation.

And that's . . . again, it's a great thing. So I really think what needs to happen is industry and government need to set goals of zero tolerance for these bugs in food and then, you know, let innovation happen. And they can happen. We're seeing the ability to trace products, you know, when we know there's a problem either through barcodes or even some really interesting innovations about putting inactive DNA in products. So if there's a, an outbreak, you can link it immediately back to where the source is. But, you know, what it really, really comes down to, in my view, to create a food safety system is to really try to simplify the number of steps so you limit the opportunity for bugs to be introduced and human error to occur.

So what's the role for public policy in this? Are there changes in policy that we need that can also help keep us safer?

There's going to be a lot more pressure on businesses to produce food potentially cheaper and, you know, we may have pressure to . . . sort of put food safety to the side.

Again, I think simplifying things as opposed to making things more complex, at least in my view, makes it easier for humans to do the right thing. Presently, you know, we have somewhere between a dozen and 20 different organizations in government that have some level of oversight for food. And it gets really difficult when you think about, you know, the cheese pizzas overseen by FDA, but cheese pizza with sausage is overseen by the USDA, and fish is overseen by FDA except for catfish, which is overseen by USDA. So one of the things that I think needs to happen, you know, is a really hard re-look at how we regulate things. You know, I think USDA has done a great job. FSIS has done a great job in how they regulate meat. FDA through the Food Safety Modernization Act is sort of taking those first steps. But part of the ongoing problem is, you know, cross-jurisdictional issues between FSIS and FDA.

You know, in a perfect world, I'd certainly like to see, you know, one single agency that was specifically charged with . . . focused on, you know, like a laser on making our food supply safe.

The Biggest Challenge

I'm wondering what you think will be the biggest food safety challenges in the decades ahead.

Well, I think it's going to be, you know . . . more food is going to be imported, so there's going to be greater distances. Either it's going to be a lot more pressure, I think, as the population gets larger. There's going to be a lot more pressure on businesses to produce food potentially cheaper and, you know, we may have pressure to, you know, sort of put food safety to the side. And I think that would be sort of wrongheaded.

So I think those are things that we really have to pay attention to make sure that *don't* happen, you know, as we're paying attention to things that come around the corner.

So you had great success with E. coli contamination cases. And since the lawsuits, there have been changes in the food system in terms of beef and improvements in health. But there doesn't seem to be the same political will today. There are still high rates of salmonella in raw chicken. It seems that there's been a challenge in passing the same types of legislation that made beef so safe.

Um, yeah. I mean, that's why I still have a job. There's certainly more to do, and if I got to be the guy with the magic wand, I would do exactly with salmonella what the government did with E. coli 20 years ago, and I would say that you can't have salmonella in chicken. And industry would adjust.

They wouldn't like it, but they would adjust. And, you know, in the long run, the industry would be better off. Consumers would be better off, and I wouldn't have anything to do.

But that's not happening yet.

Not yet.

That was William Marler, a food safety lawyer with Marler Clark. Thanks for listening to this podcast for FutureFood 2050. More information on this subject can be found at www.futurefood2050.com. I'm Cynthia Graber.

Consuming Imported Food Is Risky

Katharine Mieszkowski

Katharine Mieszkowski reports on food, water, and the environment for the website Reveal from The Center for Investigative Reporting.

Food imports are growing at a rapid rate, and federal regulators have not been able to keep up with the demand. Very little of the food that makes its way into the United States is inspected and even less is tested for dangerous bacteria. This is an alarming problem because foodborne outbreaks can be deadly. The Food and Drug Administration says it cannot do the required inspections due to a lack of funding, but it also disagrees that inspections are the best way to improve food safety. Meanwhile, problems with imported food continue to threaten the food supply.

Call it the international food movement: From blueberries to raw sushi, the tide of imported food is rising in the U.S.

Right now, about one-sixth of what Americans eat comes from outside our borders. But in recent years, food imports have grown an average of 10 percent a year, a trend that's expected to continue. Some 90 percent of our seafood, such as shrimp and tilapia fillets, comes from other countries, as well as about half of our fresh fruit. That's despite the growing popularity of farmers markets and the local food movement.

As what we eat becomes increasingly globalized, federal regulators are scrambling to prevent unsafe products from entering our borders. A new report from the U.S. Government Accountability Office casts doubt on how effective they are at keeping food imports safe.

The stakes are high, because outbreaks of foodborne illness can be deadly. In 2012, a listeriosis outbreak linked to ricotta cheese imported from Italy killed four of the 22 Americans it sickened.

Federal Regulators Struggling

Even with food grown within the U.S.'s borders, regulators struggle to prevent and curb outbreaks of foodborne illness. Food safety is such a problem that Congress and President Barack Obama are considering whether the now scattered oversight of the nation's food supply should be consolidated into one agency.

The U.S. Food and Drug Administration [FDA] has primary responsibility for overseeing the safety of most of what we eat, with notable exceptions such as meat and poultry. But that federal agency examines only about 2 percent of food imports at ports of entry and actually tests even less than that.

> *The [FDA] is failing to perform the number of inspections of foreign food facilities that they're required to do under the Food Safety Modernization Act of 2011.*

So in 2008, the FDA started opening foreign offices to help identify unsafe food, drugs and products before they make their way to the U.S. The agency now has seven of these offices around the world in China, India, Europe and Latin America. The FDA was unable to provide a budget for these foreign offices by press time.

A new report from the GAO [Government Accountability Office] said it's unclear if those offices are making our food safer. That's because the offices don't have performance measures to track and evaluate specifically how what they do improves food safety.

"We don't really know the extent to which the foreign offices are contributing to the safety of imported food," said J. Alfredo Gomez, a director on the office's natural resources and environment team.

In one area, the GAO report found that the FDA is clearly falling short. The agency is failing to perform the number of inspections of foreign food facilities that they're required to do under the Food Safety Modernization Act of 2011. "They're not following the law as currently laid out," Gomez said.

The FDA has the authority to refuse entry of food into the United States if its inspectors have not been allowed access to the foreign facilities where it was produced. But without adequate inspections, that threat doesn't really have teeth.

Plus, the agency has no plans to even try to perform all the inspections that they're mandated to do, citing budgetary constraints. FDA officials questioned the value of doing all those inspections, too, preferring instead to focus their limited resources on providing technical assistance to the food industry—both domestic and foreign—to comply with new U.S. food regulations.

The GAO report also found that the FDA's foreign offices are understaffed. Nearly half of the positions in these offices were vacant, with most of the openings in China, where the agency has had trouble getting visas from the Chinese government. The staffing problem in China is so bad that the agency sometimes relies on translators provided by the firms that they're inspecting, the report found. That could risk compromising the integrity of their findings.

FDA Believes Progress Is Being Made

Officials from the FDA's foreign offices defended their work to the General Accountability Office, citing instances where they'd made "significant contributions to determining the cause of outbreaks that lead to illnesses or deaths in the United States." For instance, the India office rapidly inspected tuna processing plants in 2012 that were potential sources of a salmonella outbreak that sickened 425 people in the U.S. in 28 different states, including 55 hospitalizations.

The FDA rejects about the same number of food imports as it did a decade ago—when imports were less than half the current level.

The Centers for Disease Control and Prevention estimates that for every documented case of salmonella poisoning, 29 cases may remain unreported, putting the likely toll of that outbreak at more like 12,325 illnesses. Eventually, Moon Marine USA Corp. of Cupertino, California, voluntarily recalled the frozen raw yellowfin tuna from India implicated in the outbreak.

Yet by the time U.S. inspectors reached the seafood company in southern India, the damage had been done, Fair Warning reported in 2014. Inspectors found "water tanks rife with microbiological contamination, rusty carving knives, peeling paint above the work area, unsanitary bathrooms and an outdoor ice machine covered with insects and 'apparent bird feces.'"

The inspectors aren't supposed to only be reactive, either. They have the ability to inspect these kinds of facilities before outbreaks; any company that wants to ship food to the United States has to agree to be inspected, or the FDA can refuse their food.

In all, Fair Warning found, the FDA rejects about the same number of food imports as it did a decade ago—when imports were less than half the current level.

The General Accountability Office made several recommendations about how the foreign offices could be improved, but it noted that it had made two of those same recommendations in another report in 2010, and the FDA had not complied with them.

A spokesperson for the FDA said the agency had no comment on the GAO report beyond its official response that is included in it. That response says the agency has made significant progress toward meeting the 2010 goals.

6

Despite Problems, the US Food System Is the Safest in the World

Grant Gerlock

Grant Gerlock is based in Lincoln, Nebraska, where he reports on agriculture and food production issues for NET News and Harvest Public Media.

There are over a dozen federal agencies involved in food safety issues, and this overcomplicates the system. Although many argue for a more streamlined system to improve food safety, the US food system is already among the safest in the world. Although perhaps unnecessarily complex, multiple agencies will continue to be involved in food safety because an overhaul of the system would be costly and is not supported by most food producers at this time.

Walking through the warehouse of food processor Heartland Gourmet in Lincoln, Neb., shows how complicated the food safety system can be. Pallets are stacked with sacks of potato flour, and the smell of fresh-baked apple-cinnamon muffins floats in the air.

Heartland Gourmet makes a wide range of foods—from muffins and organic baking mixes to pizzas and burritos. That means business manager Mark Zink has to answer to both of the main U.S. food safety regulators, the Department of Agriculture [USDA] and the Food and Drug Administration [FDA].

The product being made determines which agency is in charge. Apple-cinnamon muffins fall under the authority of the FDA. A cheese burrito or cheese pizza is also the FDA. But a beef burrito or pepperoni pizza has to meet USDA guidelines—rules formed by a totally different agency.

"[The USDA has] jurisdiction over anything with raw meat, cooked meat, anything that touches meat product," Zink explains.

The general rule of thumb: Make something with meat and the USDA is in charge. Otherwise, it's FDA.

Seafood complicates the rules, though, as the FDA has authority over seafood. But not catfish—catfish actually falls under USDA regulation.

A patchwork of more than a dozen federal agencies plays a part in keeping food from making Americans sick.

The agencies work differently. Before Zink runs a batch of beef burritos, he has to call a USDA inspector to be on-site while the food is prepared. A USDA official will stop by at other times during the year to check in. He doesn't hear from the FDA so often.

"FDA is a once-a-year thing," Zink says. "They pop in and do their inspection and they're gone."

Patchwork of Federal Agencies

A patchwork of more than a dozen federal agencies plays a part in keeping food from making Americans sick. Critics say the system has holes, and some think we would all be safer if food safety at the federal level were brought under one roof.

Altogether, 15 federal agencies play a role in food safety, from the EPA [Environmental Protection Agency] to the Centers for Disease Control [CDC]. Food processors are subject to a dizzying array of regulations, spending time and money to prove their products are safe.

Each year, 1 in 6 Americans comes down with listeria, E. coli, salmonella or some other foodborne illness. According to the CDC, 3,000 people die annually. For years, critics have said a streamlined system would be safer. Even President [Barack] Obama has called for the creation of a single food-safety agency in his 2016 budget.

Heartland Gourmet's Zink says after 25 years in the business, he has no trouble navigating the system. But there's no denying it's complex.

"And it ends up just being a gigantic mess in terms of a comprehensive approach to food safety," says Courtney Thomas, who studies political science and food safety at Virginia Tech University.

Thomas says the system looks fractured today because it was cobbled together from the start. The first food-safety laws, passed in 1906, put the USDA in charge of meat quality because the agency already worked with meatpackers. The FDA was created to ensure purity in other foods.

"Right out of the gate there were two different laws, two different legislative mandates that were given to two completely different agencies in the federal government," Thomas says. "And from there it only spiraled."

The U.S. Government Accountability Office [GAO] has been a leading critic of the fragmented food-safety system, for years labeling it a high-risk area in need of reform. The GAO's Steve Morris says the food-safety system is one recall away from a crisis.

One longstanding issue is that the various agencies tend to keep a narrow focus and work on small slices of oversight.

"Right now, what you have is fairly limited coordination," Morris says. "So the consumer and the Congress basically lack this comprehensive picture of what the national strategy is."

That's a big problem, because there are challenges ahead that cut across all agencies. For instance, 16 percent of the food Americans eat is imported, and that number is rising. Steve Taylor, a food scientist at the University of Nebraska-Lincoln, says regulators are already behind in inspecting foreign food facilities.

"And if you got to the right people in a lot of big corporations in the United States involved in food processing, they'd say that's one of their biggest worries, too," Taylor says.

One agency could be more efficient checking-in on foreign suppliers.

But Virginia Tech's Thomas says the chances are pretty low that Washington will adopt a single food-safety agency any time soon.

The U.S. food system is currently one of the safest in the world, and some say federal time and money is better spent elsewhere. Most food companies would prefer a complicated but familiar system over an unknown overhaul. And with multiple agencies involved, more politicians have oversight of food safety, which they might not want to give that up.

"There's no easy fix to this problem," Thomas says. "What you're talking about is a legal, a regulatory, and a cultural shift. A political shift that we haven't seen in this country in the last 100 years."

And without an immediate crisis, it seems there's not much political appetite for shaking up the system.

7

The US Food Safety Process Is Broken

Jason M. Breslow

Jason M. Breslow is the digital editor for the PBS series Frontline.

There are too many gaps in the food safety oversight process because the task of keeping the US food supply safe is divided between too many agencies. Although forty-eight million people become ill from foodborne illnesses annually, food companies are left on their own to develop individual risk assessment plans to reduce food contamination. In most cases, these plans are woefully inadequate, and even those plants cited for safety violations can continue to operate with little consequence.

Each year in the United States, a staggering 48 million people become sick with a foodborne illness. Roughly 128,000 end up in the hospital, and 3,000 die.

Many of those illnesses can be traced back to the meat we eat. According to the Centers for Disease Control and Prevention, 22 percent of food-related illnesses and 29 percent of deaths are attributable to meat and poultry.

On Tuesday [April 28, 2015], a new report from the Consumer Federation of America put a share of the blame on what it described as "ongoing challenges" with the U.S. Department of Agriculture's [USDA] primary food safety program.

A Failure to Develop Effective Food Safety Plans

In the U.S., meat and poultry that is sold to consumers comes with a USDA seal that reads, "inspected and passed." But as the study points out, government inspectors are not inspecting every single piece of meat that winds up in the grocery store.

The USDA's Food Safety and Inspection Service (FSIS) has more than 7,000 inspectors in meat and poultry plants across the U.S., but through an inspection program known as the Pathogen Reduction/Hazard Analysis and Critical Control Points, or PR/HACCP, companies are asked to identify for themselves points along the production chain that might leave food open to contamination. The program was originally pioneered for the relatively small amounts of food that NASA astronauts would take with them to space; meat and poultry producers later adopted it on a mass scale.

[The] gap in federal standards ... was on display in a nationwide outbreak of antibiotic-resistant salmonella that sickened 634 people across 29 states—38 percent of whom were hospitalized.

The trouble, according to the report, "is that too often plants fail to adequately design their HACCP plans," leaving the U.S. exposed to an estimated $7 billion per year in illness-related costs.

For example, the HACCP system until recently did not require plants to treat salmonella as a "hazard likely to occur" and does not currently designate specific strains of E. coli as a hazard. (E. coli 0157:H7, an illness-causing strain, does have to be accounted for.) And in cases when plants choose not to identify particular pathogens as a hazards, they are not obligated to address them.

This gap in federal standards, the report argues, was on display in a nationwide outbreak of antibiotic-resistant salmonella that sickened 634 people across 29 states—38 percent of whom were hospitalized. The outbreak was eventually linked to the California-based poultry producer Foster Farms, which had not designated salmonella as a hazard that is reasonably likely to occur—even though an investigation by the FSIS later found that nearly a quarter of poultry samples tested positive for it.

HACCP plans are submitted to the FSIS for review, but the agency is not required to approve the plans, so plants are largely free to determine what is and is not a hazard. Nonetheless, the FSIS "has repeatedly refused to consider" recommendations to approve such plans, the study notes, "saying that approval of HACCP plans goes against the 'philosophy of HACCP.'"

Another area of concern, according to the report, is that food-processing plants are frequently cited for recurring safety violations with little if any consequence.

From 2008 to 2011, for example, the FSIS issued 44,128 noncompliance records to 616 plants participating in a swine inspection pilot program. However, only 28 plants were ever suspended, despite an inspector's general report that found "some plants repeated violations as egregious as fecal matter on previously cleaned carcasses." Moreover, the inspector general found that a fifth of noncompliance reports at the 20 most cited plants were for repeat violations.

"USDA needs to provide better assurance that plants are reducing contamination of meat and poultry products and that the agency is effectively enforcing its regulations," said Chris Waldrop, the report's author and director of the Consumer Federation's Food Policy Institute. "Enforceable standards would allow the agency to take decisive action when a problem is first identified rather than after an outbreak has already occurred."

In a statement to FRONTLINE, FSIS spokesman Adam Tarr said that the agency "is continually taking steps to improve the effectiveness of HACCP, including recently requiring all poultry slaughter plants to consider salmonella to be a hazard likely to occur in their HACCP plans."

The risks in the inspection process are not going away, and regulators are unlikely to act more aggressively to close problematic plants.

Strengthened efforts on the part of the agency, Tarr added, resulted in nearly 33,000 fewer cases of salmonella from USDA-regulated products in 2014, and approximately 41,000 fewer illnesses from three major pathogens—salmonella, E. Coli 0157:H7 and listeria monocytogenes—in products regulated by FSIS.

"Overall, Americans eat 285 billion servings of meat and poultry per year and 99.99 percent of them are consumed safely," said Mark Dopp, senior vice president of regulatory affairs and general counsel for the North American Meat Institute, in a statement to FRONTLINE. The Consumer Federation report, he said, failed to highlight "many significant food safety improvements," including "a 93 percent reduction of *E. coli* O157:H7 in ground beef since 2000, significant reductions in salmonella across a majority of meat and poultry products and a greater than 80 percent reduction in listeria monocytogenes in ready-eat-meat products."

Nevertheless, lawmakers in Congress have introduced calls for more oversight of the nation's food safety. One bill, introduced jointly from Rep. Rosa DeLauro (D-Conn.) and Sen. Dick Durbin (D-Ill.) would establish a single food safety agency to consolidate the oversight that is currently shared by

15 separate government offices, including the FSIS. But passage in the face of industry pushback and turf battles among sparring agencies is far from certain.

In the meantime, said Waldrop, the risks in the inspection process are not going away, and regulators are unlikely to act more aggressively to close problematic plants.

"It takes a pretty substantial problem," said Waldrop. "They can make those threats and the plants tend to respond but it's never really a decisive action."

8

Food Suppliers Need to Examine Their Safety Programs

Bob Whitaker

Bob Whitaker is the chief science officer for the Produce Marketing Association.

The focus on passing food safety audits is misplaced. Growers shouldn't use the food safety audit requirements as their food safety program. Doing so will not make food safer because audits can be prepared for and do not reflect the daily reality in the plant. Rather, a comprehensive food safety program that includes hazard analysis should be in place and the audit should confirm that the individual plans are being followed rather than simply checking to see that the more general audit requirements are met.

I was at a grower training event on the Food Safety Modernization Act (FSMA) a while back and it was a great event with impressive participation from the growers. The speakers were wonderful and the content was carefully prepared. Over the last three years, I have probably been involved in twenty different food safety education programs aimed at helping growers build effective food safety programs. In some ways, they have been a great experience and based on feedback from the attendees, I know they have made a difference to growers and given them the information to start them down the path to building successful food safety programs. However, no matter how rewarding the events have been, I have often walked away a little frustrated. The event I attended most recently left me with the same slight feeling of frustration.

Focus on Food Safety Audits

During grower food safety events we often talk about why having a food safety program is important, how it is critical to have a program to protect your own business, protect your customers and ultimately public health. We talk about emerging science, the importance of foundational food safety programs like sanitation practices and worker hygiene and how to identify and manage potential cross contamination hazards on the farm and packinghouse. After going through this information and basically laying out the why, how and what of food safety, often some brave soul in the audience will raise their hand and ask, "So what score do I need to get in order to pass the audit?" And that's when the frustration sets in. How did passing an audit become a substitute for actually building a risk-based food safety program?

Simply developing a food safety program that supplies the paperwork required by whatever auditor is being employed does not *address the food safety needs of your company.*

So much of the food safety discussion we have in this industry is centered on passing a food safety audit. In fact for many, the food safety audit is the basis of their food safety efforts. A buyer mandates that a grower or supplier must have a food safety audit, so the goal is to pass the audit. Sounds logical enough but food safety audits don't really make food safer. This all-consuming furor over food safety audits is unfortunate because audits are only a tool, a snapshot in time, actually a snapshot in time that you get to pose for. Realistically, taking an audit is like taking an exam when you know when the exam will be scheduled, you already know all the questions that will be on the exam, and you already have all the answers too. How many of us wouldn't want to have had that situation back in high school or college? I am guessing we might have made better grades! How many times do we see a food safety recall and the report we read in the news includes a statement that says the unfortunate operation received a "superior" score on their most recent food safety audit? If you look deep in your soul, how many can say that they didn't do a little extra cleaning the day of their last food safety audit and that your operation doesn't look quite so pristine as it does during an audit? Its only human nature; we all want a good score, but how does that serve food safety?

Establishing a Food Safety Program

Minimally, food safety audits are a mechanism to demonstrate to yourself, senior management and customers that you are following *your* food safety program, and that you can verify it through your audit that day. At their best, food safety audits are excellent training opportunities for employees. Audits offer a chance to have an independent set of eyes critique your program, and are a time when you can step back from all your other responsibilities and critically look at your food safety program and how it is being implemented . . . it can be an important learning experience.

I sometimes think that if we had spent half the time we have spent as an industry over the last decade discussing how to conduct an effective hazard analysis and train producers in this art instead of wordsmithing existing food safety standards and audits and lamenting the duplicity of some of those audits, we might be better off as an industry.

Hazard analysis is really not a foreign concept to most people. People assess potential hazards and manage them in their daily lives all the time; whether we do so consciously or subconsciously. For example, when someone drives a car, they manage the risk of an accident by making sure the car is in good working order, the brakes work, it's full of gas and an effort is made to obey (at least most of the time) traffic rules and regulations to minimize the chance of an accident. When it comes to produce food safety, it is important that our food safety programs are similarly risk or hazard-based. Simply developing a food safety program that supplies the paperwork required by whatever auditor is being employed does *not* address the food safety needs of your company.

Doing a real hazard analysis does not have to be hard, but it does require personal engagement.

Doing a risk assessment does not have to be hard. Start out by making a simple line drawing. If you are a grower begin at the point you select the land you intend to grow a crop on through land preparation, planting, growing, harvesting, cooling, right up to the point where you no longer control the fate of the crop. Processors, transportation companies, distribution centers, and any other handlers can follow the same process, picking up where they impact the produce supply chain. It is important for all those who handle produce to understand the potential cross contamination hazards associated with their specific operations and adopt management strategies to minimize those risks.

As you perform your risk assessments, reach out to all the experts who are available to you for their expert advice and input on the hazards you should be considering, and how to manage them effectively. You already have lots of experts within your own organization. Who knows your operations better than the people who work for you? Too often I hear growers and processors say "just tell me what I have to do and that's what I'll do for my food safety program." How can anyone else possibly know your operations and therefore your risk profile better than you?

But see, that is where the rub is in food safety. Doing a real hazard analysis does not have to be hard, but it does require personal engagement. It's not just answering a series of published audit questions, it's taking the time and investing the human resources to review your operations, think about how the food might get contaminated, assessing what the likelihood of that contamination might be, determining how to manage that risk, determining who should be responsible for management and how you are going to verify that the risk is managed all day, every day. Since all produce operations are at least somewhat different, one size fits all approaches will never be as successful in managing contamination hazards as operation-specific hazard analysis and management programs.

In any produce company I have ever been around, there is always at least one person who knows more about his growers and their practices than anyone else. There are also usually harvest and process guys who have incredible knowledge of what they do and why. Those are the folks that can help you build an effective food safety program. Once you create a team of experts who know the science of food safety and the folks who have to live it every day and get them talking, my experience tells me that you can build an effective hazard analysis and management system and practices that mitigate risk . . . and best of all, your employees will own those practices, because they had authorship in developing them. That kind of engagement is the best tool we all have to better manage food safety risks; audits are not even close. In fact, the best kind of audit would be one that verifies the farm or packing facility or processing plant is operating in accord with the operations written hazard-based food safety plan. Too bad we can't start over and place hazard analysis first and properly use audits to verify their veracity.

9

Food Recalls Are Not Particularly Effective

James Andrews

James Andrews is a Seattle-based reporter covering science, agriculture, and foodborne illness outbreaks.

The problem with food recalls is that they occur too late—after people are already infected. The time between when someone falls ill from a serious foodborne illness and that illness is traced back to the source can be a week or more. During this time, many other people will be exposed. Additionally, if the law doesn't prohibit the identified contaminant, the farm has no legal obligation to issue a recall. Since efforts to manage foodborne illness outbreaks are inadequate, more attention should be placed on preventing contamination in the first place.

Consumers have grown accustomed to the routine of food safety recalls: A food company announces a recall after releasing a product into the market that later turns out to be contaminated with a harmful pathogen, or is otherwise faulty. The company advises customers to check the identifying numbers on the product to see if theirs is part of the recall, and, if it is, return or toss it.

However, by the time that happens, much of the affected product may already have been consumed. And, if the product causes an outbreak, it typically infects the majority of its victims before the company can issue a recall.

Given that recalls are often not issued until after the damage has been done, the question has regularly been raised in the food industry as to whether or not recalls are an effective tool in food safety. The question was the topic of a debate at this year's International Association of Food Protection (IAFP) conference in Indianapolis.

That debate featured arguments from Barbara Kowalcyk, Ph.D., CEO of the Center for Foodborne Illness Research and Prevention, and Robert Brackett, Ph.D., head of the Institute for Food Safety and Health at the Illinois Institute of Technology.

The problem with recalls is that a company usually does not even know it needs to issue a recall until a number of illness cases have been detected by healthcare providers and then linked back to a specific food product by public health professionals.

"I think recalls are absolutely an important part of a food safety plan, but they're like the airbags in a car," Brackett told *Food Safety News*. "They're a safety device you hope you never have to use."

Companies with weak food safety plans think it's OK to rely on their recall plan in the event of a contamination, but it should really be a company's very last line of defense if every other food safety measure fails, Brackett said.

The problem with recalls is that a company usually does not even know it needs to issue a recall until a number of illness cases have been detected by healthcare providers and then linked back to a specific food product by public health professionals. At best, it takes a week—but usually longer— between the time that cases are detected and a recall is initiated, Brackett said in the debate at IAFP.

Unless technology improves the speed at which outbreaks are traced to a food source, "You're always going to have this baseline majority of cases before the recall is initiated," he said.

Recalls Not Effective

Recalls are also very rarely 100-percent effective at removing a recalled product from the marketplace, Brackett said. There's always a chance that not all grocery stores will remove the recalled product, and not all consumers who purchased the product will be aware of the recall or take the time to verify whether it's affected.

While Kowalcyk agreed that food safety systems should focus on prevention, systems aren't perfect and so an effective food safety system includes an effective recall element.

According to a 2012 joint report by the United Nations Food and Agriculture Organization (FAO) and World Health Organization (WHO), food recalls minimize the impacts of food safety system failures on public health and the economy while maintaining a greater degree of public confidence in the food supply.

Kowalcyk also pointed out that the number of illnesses in outbreaks typically show a decline after recalls are initiated. She brought up a recent example of a company that was not required to issue a recall for their contaminated products.

"What is the alternative to recalls? I had actually debated just getting up here and saying two words and then sitting down," she said. "Foster Farms."

Beginning in March 2013, Foster Farms had an outbreak of Salmonella Heidelberg linked to its raw chicken. Because no laws prohibit Salmonella on raw chicken, the company was never pressured to issue a recall, and its products sickened a steady stream of a consumers for months.

Nearly a year-and-a-half later, Foster Farms issued a voluntary, limited recall, but more than 340 people were sickened in the time between when the cause of the illness was identified and when the company issued the recall.

"From a public health viewpoint, we could have potentially avoided all of those illnesses," Kowalcyk said.

And while initiating a recall costs a company an average of $10 million, the amount saved in reputation, consumer trust, and the avoidance of additional illnesses is priceless, she said.

Bracket and Kowalcyk agreed that the status quo for recalls in the American food system has plenty of room for improvement.

Finally, Brackett said, companies that issue recalls have to admit the failure of all their other food safety systems. Effective food safety tools should prevent contamination as opposed to having to react to it, he said.

Kowalcyk agreed, but said that an effective food recall could be seen as a preventive way to avoid even more illnesses caused by leaving contaminated products out in the market for longer periods.

10

The Poultry Industry Is Responsible for Many Foodborne Illnesses

Peter Walker and Felicity Lawrence

Peter Walker is a reporter and Felicity Lawrence is special correspondent on the politics of food, both for the Guardian *newspaper in London.*

Eighty percent of supermarket chickens tested in United Kingdom supermarkets in 2014 were found to contain potentially lethal bacteria. Although consumers can protect themselves by taking care in the handling and cooking of raw meat, it is up to the poultry industry to ensure the foods they produce are safe. There have been too many industry failures, including eggs contaminated with salmonella and chickens contaminated with certain types of bacteria, such as campylobacter. The poultry industry must take responsibility to secure the safety of the food supply.

A leading food expert and adviser to successive governments has called for a boycott of supermarket chicken because of "scandalous" levels of contamination after tests revealed that up to eight in 10 show traces of a potentially lethal bug.

Professor Tim Lang, who served as an expert adviser to the health and environment departments until 2011 and advised parliament on setting up the Food Standards Agency, said the levels of food poisoning bugs found in official tests on fresh retail chicken were shocking.

Eight out of 10 fresh chickens bought from UK supermarkets this summer [2014] were contaminated with the potentially lethal food-poisoning bug campylobacter, the food watchdog has said, warning that not one individual chain is meeting national targets over the issue.

Following six months of testing, an average of 70% of supermarket chickens proved positive for campylobacter on samples of skin. Within that, the Food Standards Agency [FSA] said, the more recent three months of tests from May to July showed an 80% incidence. The bug tends to be more prevalent during the summer, but consumer groups expressed shock at the soaring levels.

Across the six-month period 18% of the nearly 2,000 chickens tested contained the highest levels of campylobacter, the levels seen as most likely to make people ill. 6% of packaging showed signs of the bug.

Asda was the worst-performing retailer, with 78% of its chickens taken to labs testing positive for campylobacter over the period, followed by Co-op (73%), and then Morrison's, Sainsbury's and Waitrose, all on 69%, with Marks & Spencer showing an incidence of 67% and Tesco the best at 64%.

The industry needs to take steps to raise their game, to make strides towards reducing the burden of illness that campylobacter cause.

It is the first breakdown of the results between the various supermarket chains, the FSA said.

A collection of other retailers, taking in smaller discount chains such as Lidl, Aldi and Iceland, as well as individual retailers and butchers, had a total incidence of 76%. However,

25% of the chickens from these shops had the highest levels of contamination, the worst apart from Asda, where the figure was 28%.

Introducing the findings, Steve Wearne, director of policy for the FSA, said both retailers and the handful of giant poultry processors that serve them needed to act swiftly if they wanted to reach their official target of reducing the proportion of fresh chickens carrying the highest levels of campylobacter to 10% by the end of 2015. In the past week, the major retailers have been stepping up plans to introduce flash-freezing, steaming and new bagging methods to reduce the bug's occurrence.

The Poultry Industry Must Take Responsibly

Shoppers could still protect themselves and their families by following advice on correctly handling, storing and cooking chickens, Wearne said. However, he stressed, this was not entirely up to them. "It's not all about consumers," he said. "The industry needs to take steps to raise their game, to make strides towards reducing the burden of illness that campylobacter cause—280,000 cases each year in the UK. More needs to be done.

"We know that if the industry meets its target over the next year they will prevent tens of thousands of people each year getting ill from this really nasty bug, and will stop dozens of people each year dying from this bug and the complications it sometimes causes, and will save the UK hundreds of millions of pounds in avoiding lost productivity. We think, quite simply, that that's a target worth aiming for."

The target of no more than 10% of birds leaving processing plants with the highest levels of campylobacter was a good yardstick, Wearne said: "We want levels of campylobacter to be reduced across the board, but this focus on the most highly-contaminated birds—we know it's those which are most likely to make people ill—allows us to judge the progress that's being made."

As yet, he noted, not one major retailer was currently meeting this level, with the best, Tesco, seeing a rate of 11% for the first six months of the planned year of testing.

Wearne said: "The results show that wherever you buy chicken from it might have campylobacter on it, and that no individual retailer, nor the industry as a whole, is yet meeting the targets we have agreed."

The food industry and poultry trade in particular have failed to get a grip of this totally unacceptable situation.

Asked what processors and retailers were doing, Wearne said they depended on a range of factors. Among the "a la carte menu of interventions" included better bio-security and more changes of overalls and boots between sheds at farms, better processes for eviscerating birds at processing plants, and innovations in stores such as leak-proof packaging and roast-in-the-bag chickens, stopping consumers from having to handle the raw meat.

"It will require—it does require—material investment," he said. "And we know from talking to the retailers and processors that it's in the order of millions of pounds. But the public health gains are extremely significant."

More Industry Failures

Writing on the *Guardian*'s website, Professor Lang says the FSA findings on dirty chicken are on a par with previous food scandals over salmonella in eggs and BSE [bovine spongiform encephalopathy, or mad cow disease] in cattle.

"It is now clear that the food industry and poultry trade in particular have failed to get a grip of this totally unacceptable situation . . . essentially they have been continuing to trade while, and perhaps even by, selling contaminated food. The FSA has not been getting a grip of this poisonous mix either." The public should "be outraged and withhold their money until they can have confidence in what they consume", he added.

The consumer watchdog Which? was also scathing about the industry's "scandalous" performance on campylobacter, saying "supermarket bosses should hang their heads in shame" over their results.

The Consumers Association, meanwhile, said much more needed to be done and supermarket bosses should "hang their head in shame". "These results are a damning indictment of supermarkets and consumers will be rightly shocked at the failure of trusted household brands to stem the tide of increasingly high levels of campylobacter," said Richard Lloyd from the organisation.

The largest poultry processor, 2 Sisters, which supplies chicken to several of the leading supermarkets including Tesco, Sainsbury's, Morrisons, the Co-op, M&S, and Aldi, called for a "proportionate" response. "Unnecessary overreaction around this issue [has] the potential to cause undue alarm for consumers and consequently damage the UK's food and farming industries," it said. It added that it had pledged £10m [million] to reduce campylobacter and was working hard with retailers and farms on the problem.

Tackling the Problem

All the supermarket groups said they were working to tackle the contamination with a variety of measures. An Asda spokesperson said: "We take campylobacter seriously and it goes without saying that we're disappointed with these findings. There is no 'silver bullet' to tackle this issue, but along with other retailers, we're working hard to find a solution.

"We have led the industry in packaging innovation and were the first supermarket to launch roast-in-the-bag chicken, removing the need to handle raw meat." Asda is trialling a new procedure, SonoSteam, which, if successful, will be rolled out across its suppliers.

The British Retail Consortium said it would be working even harder to find solutions to help consumers such as leak-proof packaging for all raw chicken and new roast-in-the-bag products.

All producers and retailers have levels [of campylobacter] in the same range. This reinforces how universal and challenging the issue is and the complex nature of campy-lobacter.

The consortium's director of food and sustainability said: "There has been concern that implementing a solution to prevent campylobacter will mean the cost of chicken increases but we believe any increase should be small, and in our competitive market retailers will work with their suppliers to do everything they can to avoid passing this on to consumers."

The British Poultry Council said: "The data released from six months of sampling shows that all producers and retailers have levels in the same range. This reinforces how universal and challenging the issue is and the complex nature of campy-lobacter.

"Poultry producers have looked at every part of their production chain to see where new ideas and technology can combat this very complex bacteria: improved biosecurity on farms, new methods in the slaughterhouse, and brand new technologies being developed such as SonoSteam, rapid surface chilling, and roast-in-the-bag packaging. We hope that a combination of these measures will, over time, reduce the level of campylobacter in chickens."

Campylobacter Q&A

What is campylobacter?

Campylobacter is a nasty food-poisoning bug that thrives in the gut and faeces of all kinds of poultry and can cause infections in humans.

What's the problem with chickens?

Up to 80% of cases of campylobacter food poisoning in humans may be attributable to contaminated raw chicken.

How serious is it?

Campylobacter makes around 280,000 people sick and causes approximately 100 deaths each year in the UK, although the figure for illness is probably much higher since most people do not report milder cases of food poisoning.

How much chicken is contaminated?

Eighty per cent of fresh whole chickens in supermarkets and butchers were contaminated in tests over the summer months from May to June. The average rate of contamination over six months, February to July, was 70%.

Is there any safe level of campylobacter?

No, any level can make you sick but the higher the rate of contamination, the more likely it is to make you sick. One-fifth of retail chicken tested fell into the heavily contaminated category.

The [campylobacter] bug is killed by cooking but can easily be spread from raw chicken.

Is it illegal to sell chicken contaminated with campylobacter?

No, the industry is required to remove from sale foods that test positive for salmonella, but are not restricted in selling campylobacter-contaminated food.

Is it safe to buy chicken?

The bug is killed by cooking but can easily be spread from raw chicken. The FSA advises consumers not to wash chicken before cooking as that can spread the bacteria around the kitchen, to double-wrap raw chicken to keep it separate from other food in the fridge, to throw away shopping bags that become contaminated with raw juice, to wash anything chicken comes in to contact with thoroughly, including hands, surfaces and utensils, and to cook chicken well. Freezing also kills the bug.

Are there safer places to buy chicken?

All major supermarkets have unacceptable levels of campylobacter contamination on their fresh chicken, ranging from around two-thirds of birds contaminated for the best performers, to four-fifths of their birds carrying campylobacter in the worst. No retailer is meeting the official target of having less than 10% of its chickens heavily contaminated. In the UK, 90% of fresh chickens come from the intensive farms and abattoirs of just five processing companies.

Is there much difference between retailers?

Asda tested as having 78% of chickens contaminated, with 28% heavily contaminated, and was above average, while Tesco chickens tested as 64% contaminated with 11% heavily contaminated and was below average. All the other major retailers had rates of contamination in between.

What might account for the difference?

The FSA says retailers drive standards in their specifications to suppliers so they will be key to improving the figures.

Is there any difference between top of the range and bargain special offer chickens or intensive and free range/organic?

No, and they often come from the same abattoirs anyway.

11

Reports of Illnesses from Fruit and Vegetables Are Overblown

National Health Service

The National Health Service is the publicly funded health-care system for the United Kingdom.

News outlets reporting that eating plenty of fruits and vegetables increases your chance of getting food poisoning are lacking accurate information. The study they cite in these articles does not support their claims. Instead, the study suggests that most food poisoning occurs in the home from not using proper hygiene and cooking techniques. While the data provided in the research is alarming, it doesn't mean that anyone should stop eating fresh produce.

Can fruit and vegetables be dangerous? The *Mail Online* seems to think so. A story published on the website warns that: "Getting your five a day is responsible for half of all food poisoning cases."

The story comes from a decade-long US study of the sources of foodborne illnesses in the US. It estimates that nearly half of all foodborne illnesses were caused by fruit, nuts and vegetables, particularly green leafy vegetables. Meat and poultry accounted for around one in five cases.

The study highlights the important fact that any foodstuff, if it is improperly prepared or stored, can cause food poisoning.

The germs responsible for these illnesses attributed to leafy vegetables commonly include E. coli and the winter vomiting bug, *norovirus*. These highly contagious germs are often spread "hand-to-mouth" (usually through not washing hands properly after going to the toilet).

However, these results do not mean that fruit and vegetables are bad for you, only that it is crucial to have high standards of personal and food hygiene.

A more useful headline would have explained the cause of the problem—poorly prepared, handled or stored fruit and vegetables can lead to food poisoning.

There are rules covering the hygiene requirements of environments and personnel involved in the preparation and handling of food in the UK.

Meanwhile, in the home there are many ways you can help to stay safe, including washing your hands before handling and eating food, thoroughly washing raw fruit, vegetables and salads before eating, taking care over the storage of food and ensuring that meat for your weekend barbecue is thoroughly cooked. . . .

CDC Research

The study was carried out by researchers from the US Centers for Disease Control and Prevention [CDC], which is funded by the US government. The study was published in the peer-reviewed open-access journal *Emerging Infectious Diseases*.

The *Mail Online*'s headline appears to be confusing and perversely scaremongering, as it implies that eating five portions of fruit and vegetables increases your risk of food poisoning—a claim that is not supported by the study. A more useful headline would have explained the cause of the problem—poorly prepared, handled or stored fruit and vegetables can lead to food poisoning.

This frankly silly type of headline writing is a shame as the actual article is very well written and should be congratulated for highlighting the often ignored issue of "fruit and veg" associated food poisoning.

In this study, researchers aimed to calculate which specific foods and food groups were responsible for food poisoning outbreaks reported in the US between 1998 and 2008. They used this information to estimate the foods chiefly responsible for foodborne illness.

The authors point out that, despite advances in food safety, more than 9 million people suffer food poisoning in the US each year.

They say that one challenge in preventing foodborne illness is to decide where to prioritise food safety efforts, when a number of different foods may be involved (such as meat, fish or salad).

Attributing all illnesses to specific foods is challenging because most food pathogens are transmitted through a variety of foods and linking an illness to a particular food is rarely possible except during an outbreak.

During 1998–2008, a total of 13,352 foodborne disease outbreaks, causing 271,974 illnesses, were reported in the US.

Food poisoning can be caused by a range of different pathogens. These include bacteria (such as salmonella and E. coli), viruses (such as norovirus, known as the "winter vomiting" bug), chemicals, and parasites (such as cryptosporidium). In the UK, most cases of food poisoning are caused by bacteria or viruses.

Most cases of food poisoning are not serious, although they are usually unpleasant. Complications can occur in more vulnerable people, such as older people, and they may require admission to hospital, for example due to dehydration.

It is estimated that in the UK, food poisoning is to blame for 20,000 hospitalisations and 500 deaths every year.

For their study, the researchers used data on food poisoning outbreaks in the US reported to the US Centers for Disease Control and Prevention (CDC) from state and local health departments, through an established surveillance system.

These reports include the number of people taken ill, the suspected or confirmed cause of the outbreak (the pathogen or "bug"), the implicated food "vehicle" (the meal that caused the poisoning) and the identity of contaminated ingredients in that food.

They say that during 1998–2008, a total of 13,352 foodborne disease outbreaks, causing 271,974 illnesses, were reported in the US. Of these, they looked at 4,887 (37%) which were attributed to a particular food "vehicle" (source) and a single cause. They excluded 298 of these outbreaks because not enough information about the food "vehicle" was provided to categorise ingredients.

They obtained data on the estimated number of illnesses, hospitalisations and deaths for each outbreak.

The researchers then created 17 mutually exclusive food groups or "commodities":

- three for aquatic animals (fish, crustaceans and molluscs)

- six for land animals (dairy, eggs, beef, game, pork and poultry)

- eight for plants (grains and beans, oils and sugars, fruits and nuts, fungi, and leafy, root and vine-stalk vegetables)

They also divided foods into those that were "simple" containing ingredients from one group or commodity only (such as apple juice or fruit salad), and "complex" containing ingredients from more than one commodity, such as apple pie (made from fruit, flour, sugar and dairy).

They then calculated the proportion of outbreak-associated illnesses transmitted by each food commodity, taking account of whether foods involved in the outbreaks were complex or simple. They then applied the percentages they derived from the data to the 9.6 million estimated annual illnesses in the US caused by food poisoning. They provided a range of estimates, using the most probable estimates in their results.

Research Results

The researchers included 4,589 food poisoning outbreaks and 120,321 cases of food poisoning in their study. They found that norovirus (the most common cause of diarrhoea and vomiting in the UK and elsewhere) caused the most outbreaks (1,419) and illnesses (41,257) in the US during the period analysed.

Causes of foodborne illness

- plant commodities—fruits, nuts and vegetables—accounted for 46% of foodborne illnesses

- meat and poultry accounted for 22% of illnesses

- among all 17 commodities, more illnesses were attributable to leafy vegetables (2.2 million or 22%) than any other commodity

- after leafy vegetables, commodities linked to the most illnesses were dairy (1.3 million 14%), fruits and nuts (1.1 million, 12%), and poultry (900,000, 10%)

Hospitalisations for food poisoning

- 46% (26,000) of annual hospitalisations were attributed to meat and dairy (land animals)

- 41% (24,000) were attributed to plant foods

- 6% (3,000) were attributed to fish and other seafood (aquatic animals)

- dairy foods accounted for the most hospitalisations, followed by leafy vegetables, poultry and vine stalk vegetables

Deaths from food poisoning

- an estimated 43% (629) deaths each year were attributed to meat (land animals), 363 (25%) to plant foods and 94 (6%) to fish and other seafood (aquatic animals)

- poultry accounted for the most deaths (19%) followed by dairy (10%), vine stalk vegetables (7%), fruit-nuts (6%) and leafy vegetables (6%)

This large study of the possible sources of food poisoning in the US over a ten year period comes from a reputable source.

They also say that plant foods accounted for 66% of viral illness, 32% of bacterial, 25% of chemical and 30% of parasitic illness.

The researchers point out that more illnesses were attributed to leafy vegetables (22%) than to any other commodity. In addition, illnesses associated with leafy vegetables were the second most frequent cause of hospitalisations (14%) and the fifth most frequent cause of death (6%). Efforts are particularly needed to prevent contamination of plant foods and poultry, they argue.

Reducing the Risk

This large study of the possible sources of food poisoning in the US over a ten year period comes from a reputable source.

However, as the authors point out, it can only give estimates as to the sources of food poisoning and it is also based on data before and up to 2008.

Since that time, patterns of food poisoning and the agents which cause it, may have changed. Also, its calculations are based on only a third of all food poisoning outbreaks in the US during the ten years covered.

It should also be noted that the findings may not apply to food poisoning trends in the UK.

Nevertheless, the findings of the study are of concern and a timely reminder of the crucial importance of food hygiene. The germs responsible for these illnesses attributed to leafy vegetables mostly include those highly contagious germs that are most often spread from the hand to the mouth, especially if you haven't washed your hands properly after going to the toilet.

While this study did not explore the causes of these outbreaks, the vegetables would have most likely been contaminated by the hands of people carrying these bacteria at any stage along the line of production, processing or preparation.

There are high standards covering the hygiene requirements of environments and personnel involved in the preparation and handling of food in the UK. And ensuring food is safe to eat is a legal responsibility of both those involved in food production and processing. However, you should be wary of being complacent about food hygiene.

You can reduce your risk by:

- always washing your hands before handling and eating food

- thoroughly washing raw fruit, vegetables and salads before eating

- ensuring produce such as fresh produce doesn't come into contact with raw meat

- ensuring that meat is thoroughly cooked

- when reheating items ensure that they are thoroughly heated through

- ensuring that meats, fish, dairy products and prepared meals are refrigerated, and not left standing in the room or outside (in hot temperatures, the time after which such food will become unsafe to eat will be less)

- observing use-by dates

12

Poor Animal Welfare Increases Foodborne Illness

Paige M. Tomaselli

Paige M. Tomaselli practices law in the San Francisco Bay area.

So-called ag-gag laws that criminalize would-be whistle-blowers endanger the food supply. When animals are kept in unsanitary conditions, become ill, and then enter the food supply, bacteria outbreaks are likely to occur. The best place for these problems to be identified is inside the farms and processing plants. The US Department of Agriculture cannot keep tabs on all farms at all times, so having help from those inside the industry is an important way to keep the food supply safe.

In March [2014], Center for Food Safety, along with a coalition of animal protection, labor rights, and environmental groups, filed a federal lawsuit to overturn Idaho's new "ag-gag" statute, which was signed into law on February 28, 2014. The statute criminalizes whistle-blowing activities on factory farms and slaughterhouses, including audio and video recordings of animal welfare violations without the farm owner's permission. Anyone convicted of this conduct can face up to a year in prison or a $5,000 fine.

Last Thursday [April 3, 2014], the state of Idaho filed a Motion to Dismiss the case, essentially arguing that its interest in protecting animal factories is greater than its interest in protecting consumers. This backward way of thinking seriously jeopardizes public health. Here's why:

Ag-gag Laws and Food Safety

Opponents of ag-gag laws are often portrayed as solely concerned with animal welfare. While animal welfare is a serious problem, ag-gag laws also present a threat to food safety by seeking to stop investigative activities that could keep contaminated food off the market. Three thousand consumers are killed and 48.7 million are sickened each year from ingesting foodborne pathogens. Beef, poultry, and eggs are the worst offenders. In 2009 and 2010, eggs tainted with Salmonella were responsible for the most food-related illnesses, and beef and poultry were ranked as the first and fourth commodities most often associated with pathogen outbreaks.

When federal agencies fail, private investigations like those banned by ag-gag laws can be the only way to prevent contaminated meat and eggs from entering the food supply.

Now consider that by some estimates, 99% of chickens and 78% of beef are raised and slaughtered in animal factory facilities, which ag-gag laws seek to protect. The conditions in which these animals are kept and processed before hitting your plate are critical to maintaining a healthy food supply, but often times these animals live in unsanitary and cramped surroundings. Animals that are forced to stand or lay in close quarters are extremely likely to contact fecal matter. Every year, an estimated 195,000 to 1.8 million cows collapse in factory farm facilities, becoming "downer" cows. These cows are susceptible to Salmonella and E.coli contamination not only because they are in constant contact with animal waste, but because they are often under extreme stress and cannot access food, reducing their ability to fight infection. If these cattle are permitted to enter the food supply, an alarmingly common occurrence, consumers are put at risk.

Similarly, inhumane treatment of chickens before slaughter increases the likelihood they will come in contact with pathogens. Animal factory-raised hens have been known to live covered in manure, walked through manure trenches and across manure-coated floors. Often, the hens will come into contact with egg conveyer belts, exposing the eggs to fecal bacteria. Dead birds are customarily left in and around cages with live hens and near eggs.

These serious threats to food safety occur in facilities that are supposedly being monitored by the USDA [US Department of Agriculture]. When federal agencies fail, private investigations like those banned by ag-gag laws can be the only way to prevent contaminated meat and eggs from entering the food supply. In 2007, an investigator for the Humane Society of the United States documented "egregious" violations of federal regulations at the Hallmark/Westland slaughtering plant. The investigator filmed downer cows being pushed with heavy machinery, electrically shocked, and finally dragged to slaughter. As a result of this investigation, USDA Food Safety and Inspection Service officials admitted they often took shortcuts when inspecting cattle before slaughter. This led to one of the largest beef recalls in U.S. history. In 2009, a hidden camera in a veal slaughtering plant documented a USDA inspector's failure to shut down the plant after witnessing a worker attempt to skin a live calf that had somehow ended up with the slaughtered calves.

The welfare of animals raised and slaughtered in animal factories has a direct correlation with the safety of the U.S. food supply. Today, even after these well documented examples of potential threats to the food supply, Congress has proposed regulations that would reduce the number of USDA officials conducting on-site inspections of animal factory facilities. Ag-gag laws like Idaho's new statute seek to criminalize one of the last lines of defense against foodborne pathogens in the U.S. meat supply. We won't let that happen.

Organizations to Contact

The editors have compiled the following list of organizations concerned with the issues debated in this book. The descriptions are derived from materials provided by the organizations. All have publications or information available for interested readers. The list was compiled on the date of publication of the present volume; the information provided here may change. Be aware that many organizations take several weeks or longer to respond to inquiries, so allow as much time as possible.

Academy of Nutrition and Dietetics, Home Food Safety
120 South Riverside Plaza, Suite 2000, Chicago, IL   60606
(800) 877-1600
e-mail: HFS@eatright.org
website: homefoodsafety.org

The Academy of Nutrition and Dietetics is the world's largest organization of food and nutrition professionals. The group strives to improve the nation's health and advance the profession of dietetics through research, education, and advocacy. The organization focuses on food and nutrition research and offers scholarships and awards. Its website, EatRight.org, contains numerous papers on managing a healthy, nutritionally sound diet. To raise consumer awareness about the seriousness of food poisoning the Academy also provides the website HomeFoodSafety.org to offer guidance for safely handling food in home kitchens. HomeFoodSafety.org also provides safety statistics and additional general information about food poisoning.

American Society for Nutrition (ASN)
9650 Rockville Pike, Bethesda, MD   20814
(301) 634-7050
e-mail: info@nutrition.org
website: www.nutrition.org

The American Society for Nutrition (ASN) is a nonprofit organization dedicated to bringing together the world's top researchers, clinical nutritionists, and industry to advance our knowledge and application of nutrition. ASN supports its members and fulfills its mission in a number of ways, including fostering and enhancing research in animal and human nutrition; providing opportunities for sharing, disseminating, and archiving peer-reviewed nutrition research results; and fostering quality education and training in nutrition.

Centers for Disease Control and Prevention (CDC)
1600 Clifton Rd., Atlanta, GA   30333
(800) 232-4636
website: www.cdc.gov

As the health protection agency of the United States, the Centers for Disease Control and Prevention (CDC) promotes health and the prevention of disease, injury, and disability. To accomplish this mission, CDC conducts critical research and provides health information to members of the healthcare and public-safety community. The CDC website includes consumer health information on lifestyle diseases, such as heart disease and diabetes, as well as information about food safety and diet.

Health Canada
Tower A, Qualicum Towers, 2936 Baseline Rd.
Ottawa   K1A OK9
  Canada
(866) 225-0709
website: www.hc-sc.gc.ca

Health Canada is the federal department responsible for helping Canadians maintain and improve their health. Health Canada relies on high-quality scientific research and conducts ongoing consultations with Canadians to determine long-term health-care needs. Health Canada encourages Canadians to take an active role in their health and issues publications, including *Canada's Food Guide to Healthy Eating*. Its website also contains a section on food safety with general tips for handling food safely and information on current food recalls.

National Institutes of Health (NIH)

9000 Rockville Pike, Bethesda, MD   20892
(301) 496-4000
e-mail: NIHinfo@od.nih.gov
website: www.nih.gov

The National Institutes of Health (NIH) is the largest source of funding for medical research in the world, funding thousands of scientists in universities and research institutions in every state across America and around the globe. NIH is divided into twenty-seven institutes and centers, each with a specific research agenda. The Institute of Diabetes and Digestive and Kidney Diseases presents information on its website about foodborne illnesses, including transmission and prevention and complications of infection. The Institute also publishes current statistics on foodborne illness outbreaks.

US Department of Agriculture (USDA), Food and Nutrition Service

3101 Park Center Dr., 10th Floor, Alexandria, VA   22302
(703) 305-7600
website: www.fns.usda.gov

The Food and Nutrition Service (FNS) of the US Department of Agriculture (USDA) works to end hunger and obesity through the administration of federal nutrition assistance programs, including school meals. The FNS Office of Food Safety website provides food safety education and training resources for school food service professionals and child nutrition program operators.

US Department of Health and Human Services FoodSafety.gov

200 Independence Ave. SW, Washington, DC   20201
(877) 696-6775
website: http://foodsafety.gov

The Foodsafety.gov website is provided by the Office of Disease Prevention and Health Promotion within the US Department of Health and Human Services. The website provides food safety information from various government agencies, including the Food Safety and Inspection Service, the Food and Drug Administration, and Centers for Disease Control and Prevention. The website also exists as a place to report suspected cases of food poisoning, while it offers reports on food safety recalls and tips for handling food safely.

US Environmental Protection Agency (EPA)

1200 Pennsylvania Ave. NW, Washington, DC   20460
(202) 272-0167
website: www.epa.gov

The mission of the US Environmental Protection Agency (EPA) is to ensure that all Americans are protected from significant risks to human health and the environment where they live, learn, and work. The EPA develops and enforces regulations, gives grants, studies environmental issues, forms sponsor partnerships, teaches people about the environment, and publishes related information via its website. Additionally, updated information about government food safety programs, research and technology available to food producers and processers, and fish food advisories are available at its website.

US Food and Drug Administration (FDA)

5100 Paint Branch Pkwy., College Park, MD   20740
(888) 463-6332
website: www.fda.gov

The US Food and Drug Administration (FDA) is the government agency responsible for ensuring the quality and safety of all food and drug products sold in the United States. As such, the FDA regulates safety and truthful labeling of all food products, including dietary supplements (except for livestock and poultry, which are regulated by the US Department of Agriculture), venison and other game meat, bottled water, food additives, and infant formulas. FDA reports as well as current information on food quality issues are available at its website.

World Health Organization (WHO)

Avenue Appia 20, Geneva 27   1211
   Switzerland
+41 22 791 21 11
website: www.who.int

The role of the World Health Organization (WHO) is to direct and coordinate international health within the United Nations' system. WHO helps countries coordinate the efforts of multiple sectors of the government and partners to attain their health objectives and support their national health policies and strategies. Every year, WHO selects a priority area of global public health concern as the theme for World Health Day. Food safety was the area selected for 2015 and as such special coverage for retailers and the public is available at its website.

Bibliography

Books

Charlotte Biltekoff	*Eating Right in America: The Cultural Politics of Food & Health*. Durham, NC: Duke University Press, 2013.
Michael Booth and Jennifer Brown	*Eating Dangerously: Why the Government Can't Keep Your Food Safe . . . and How You Can*. Summit, PA: Rowman & Littlefield, 2014.
Charles M. Duncan	*Eat, Drink, & Be Wary*. Summit, PA: Rowman & Littlefield, 2015.
David E. Gumpert	*The Raw Milk Revolution: Behind America's Emerging Battle over Food Rights*. White River Junction, VT: Chelsea Green Publishing, 2009.
Richard Hyde	*Regulating Food-Borne Illness*. Oxford, UK: Hart Publishing, 2015.
Jayson Lusk	*The Food Police: A Well-Fed Manifesto About the Politics of Your Plate*. New York: Crown Forum, 2013.
Denise Minger	*Death By Food Pyramid: How Shoddy Science, Sketchy Politics and Shady Special Interests Have Ruined Our Health*. Malibu, CA: Primal Blueprint, 2014.
Marion Nestle	*Safe Food: Bacteria, Biotechnology, and Bioterrorism*. Oakland: University of California Press, 2010.

Robert L. Paarlberg — *Food Politics: What Everyone Needs to Know.* New York: Oxford University Press, 2010.

John Robbins — *The Food Revolution: How Your Diet Can Help Save Your Life and Our World.* San Francisco: Conari Press, 2010.

Morton Satin — *Death in the Pot: The Impact of Food Poisoning on History.* Amherst, NY: Prometheus Books, 2007.

Eric Schlosser — *Fast Food Nation: The Dark Side of the All-American Meal.* Boston: Houghton Mifflin Harcourt, 2012.

Courtney I.P. Thomas — *In Food We Trust: The Politics of Purity in American Food Regulation.* Lincoln: University of Nebraska Press, 2014.

David Vogel — *The Politics of Precaution: Regulating Health, Safety, and Environmental Risks in Europe and the United States.* Princeton, NJ: Princeton University Press, 2012.

Melanie Warner — *Pandora's Lunchbox: How Processed Food Took Over the American Meal.* New York: Scribner, 2013.

Keith Woodford — *Devil in the Milk: Illness, Health and the Politics of A1 and A2 Milk.* White River Junction, VT: Chelsea Green Publishing, 2009.

Periodicals and Internet Sources

ABC News "How Safe Are School Lunches?,"
November 7, 2014.
http://abcnews.go.com.

Katie Amey "The Foods to Avoid on Your
Summer Holiday," *Daily Mail*, June
19, 2015.

Linda Carroll "9 out of 10 Preschoolers' Lunches
Reach Unsafe Temperatures," *Today
Health*, August 8, 2011.
www.today.com.

Grace Chen "Why Fast Food Is 'Healthier' Than
School Lunches: The Shocking USDA
Truth," *Public School Review*, June 16,
2015. www.publicschoolreview.com.

Carmen Chi "Food Safety: Are Food-Borne
Illnesses, Recalls on the Rise in
Canada?," *Global News*, June 1, 2015.

Consumer Reports "Prevent Food Poisoning from
Listeria Bacteria," June 5, 2015.

Bennie DiNardo "Food Trucks as Safe as Restaurants,
Study Says," *Boston Globe*, June 2014.

Food Safety News "Wisconsin Bill Requires Food
Protection Certificates for School
Lunch," March 25, 2015.

Carolyn
Heneghan "Could Faster Listeria Testing Reduce
Massive Recalls?," *Food Dive*, May 29,
2015. www.fooddive.com.

Clare
Leschin-Hoar

"A New Addition to the School Lunch Menu: E. Coli," *Take Part*, April 9, 2013. www.takepart.com.

Bill Marler

"If You Are a Manufacturer of Adulterated Food Can You Face Fines and Jail?," *Forbes*, June 9, 2015.

Carl Nierenberg

"6 Potential Dangers of Juice Cleanses and Liquid Diets," *LiveScience*, November 24, 2014. www.livescience.com.

Tom Philpott

"4 Foods That Could Disappear if New Food Safety Rules Pass," *Mother Jones*, November 6, 2013.

Joanna Plucinska

"China Seizes Rotting 40-Year-Old Meat Destined for Dinner Tables," *Time*, June 24, 2015.

Christine Sarkis

"10 Foods You Should Never Eat Overseas," Smarter Travel, June 18, 2015. www.smartertravel.com.

David Shamah

"A Zap a Day Keeps Listeria Away, Research Shows," *Times of Israel*, June 4, 2015.

Alexandra
Sifferlin

"12 Recalled Foods Not to Eat This Week," *Time*, March 27, 2015.

Kimberly Lord
Steward

"Is Jail Time the Solution to America's Food Safety Problem?," Eater.com, June 18, 2015. www.eater.com.

Lydia Wheeler

"FDA Moves to Finalize Food Safety Rules," *The Hill*, June 11, 2015.

Rick Windham   "Food Safety Is a Concern for Summertime Camping," *Beatrice Daily Sun*, May 27, 2015.

Index

CPSIA information can be obtained
at www.ICGtesting.com
Printed in the USA
BVOW06s2123081217
502255BV00008B/63/P